Inca, Aztec, Maya Activity Book

Authors	Mary Jo Keller
	Linda Milliken
Editor	Kathy Rogers
Illustrator	Barb Lorseyedi
Cover Design	Imaginings

METRIC CONVERSION CHART

Refer to this chart when metric conversions are not found within the activity.

¼ tsp =	1 ml	350° F =	180° C
½ tsp =	2 ml	375° F =	190° C
1 tsp =	5 ml	400° F =	200° C
1 Tbsp =	15 ml	425° F =	216° C
¼ cup =	60 ml	1 inch =	2.54 cm
⅓ cup =	80 ml	1 foot =	30 cm
½ cup =	125 ml	1 yard =	91 cm
1 cup =	250 ml	1 mile =	1.6 km
1 oz. =	28 g		
1 lb. =	.45 kg		

©1999 Edupress, Inc. • P.O. Box 883 • Dana Point, CA 92629
www.edupressinc.com

ISBN 1-56472-150-7
Printed in USA

Table of Contents

Literature List

• *The Incas (See Through History Series)*
by Tim Wood;
Viking 1996. (4-6)
Readers discover the secrets of Inca civilization
and peel back the double-page acetates to look
inside a typical Inca house, a temple to the sun
god, an emperor's palace, and a messenger's
roadside station.

• *Aztec, Inca & Maya (Eyewitness Books)*
by Elizabeth Baquedano;
Knopf 1993. (3-5)
Captioned full-color photographs highlight a
close-up look at three ancient civilizations,
discussing the artistic, scientific, and technical
achievements of the Inca, Maya, and Aztec
peoples.

• *The Maiden of the Andes (Time Travelers)*
by Janet Buell;
Twenty First Century Books 1997. (4-7)
Focuses on the science of forensics, which was the
key to unraveling secrets about the ancient Incas of
Peru. It begin with the discovery of the mummy of
a young girl frozen in the Andes.

• *Gods and Goddesses of the Ancient Maya*
by Leonard Everett Fisher;
Holiday House 1999. (4-8)
Information about the lives, culture, and beliefs of
the ancient Mayas is presented through the
introduction of twelve major Mayan deities.

• *The Aztec Indians (Junior Library of American
Indians)*
by Victoria Sherrow;
Chelsea House Publishing 1993. (4-6)
Chronicles the history of the once magnificent
civilization, focusing on such achievements as
their temples, unique art, and picture writing, and
examining the cultural inheritance they they
bequeathed to modern Mexico.

• *The Aztecs (Look into the Past)*
by Peter Hicks;
Thomson Learning 1993. (3-5)
Examines the history, work, family life, and
culture of the Aztecs.

• *The Ancient Aztecs: Secrets of a Lost
Civilization, to Unlock and Discover*
by Fiona MacDonald;
Running Press 1996. (5-8)
Fully illustrated guide offers insights into daily
life in Mexico and in the golden age of Aztec
rule in the 15th century.

• *The Aztec News*
by Philip Steele, Penny Bateman, Norma
Rosso;
Candlewick Press 1997. (3-6)
Provides a fact-filled introduction to the life and
times of the Aztec people, including sports,
politics, and religion, in a creative newspaper-
style presentation.

• *The Grandchildren of the Incas*
by Ritva Lehtinen and Karl E. Nurmi;
Carolrhoda LB 1991. (4-6)
Some children herd sheep while others work in
the city in this profile of young Incan
descendants.

• *The Aztecs (Journey into Civilization)*
by Robert Nicholson, Claire Watts;
Chelsea House Publishing 1994. (3-6)
An introduction to the history of the Aztec
civilization.

• *Mayan Folktales: Folklore from Lake
Atitlan, Guatemala*
by James D. Sexton (translator);
University of New Mexico Press 1999. (4-7)
A collection of stories from the Mayan mythic
heritage that contains tales about witches,
shamans, spiritualists, and other beings that
inhabit the Mayan upper and underworlds.

• *The Corn Grows Ripe*
by Dorothy Rhoads;
Puffin 1993. (3-7)
When his father is badly injured in an accident,
a young Mayan boy wonders who will plant and
harvest the corn that they need to survive—and
to please the Mayan gods.

Introduction

When European explorers came to Latin America in the 15th century, they were surprised to find evidence of vast civilizations in the land they meant to conquer. In their pursuit of land and their search for mineral wealth they came across the ruins of the great Mayan civilization, as well as the existence of the thriving cities of the Aztec and Incan nations. Although these great civilizations were not to survive the European invasion, their influence can be seen even today.

The Maya—250 to 900 AD

For about fifteen centuries the people known as the Maya lived in the thick jungles and lowlands of Mexico and Central America. During the height of its civilization, from 250 AD to 900 AD, Maya culture spread over 125,000 square miles (325,00 sq km). Their territory broke into three separate parts. The northern section was in the Yucatan Peninsula. The central part stretched from the Gulf of Mexico in the west to the Caribbean Sea in the east. It included parts of Mexico and the northern part of Guatemala. The third part included the highlands and plateaus of southern Guatemala and a small northern corner of Honduras and El Salvador.

The earliest days of the Mayan civilization date from about 2500 BC. It began as simple farming communities made up of a few families surrounded by their fields. Each family lived in its own small compound. There were no social classes, no temples or public buildings. As the population increased, the settlements grew to include many more families, larger houses, and many public buildings.

During the peak of the Mayan civilization there were vast cities with huge pyramids topped by majestic temples. There were palaces and roads. A system of writing and an amazingly accurate calendar were developed. Then suddenly and strangely, about 900 AD, the culture collapsed. By the time the explorer Christopher Columbus made a visit to Mayan lands in 1502 AD, the once-great Mayan cities were deserted and the people were scattered throughout the countryside.

The Inca—1438 to 1532 AD

The Inca were a South American civilization that began to flourish around 1438. They settled in Cuzco, in the area that is now Peru, and began to expand their empire outward. Over the next one hundred years, their lands stretched more than 2,170 miles (3,500 km) from north to south along the western edge of South America. Over six million people were ruled by a strong ruler, the Tapa Inca, who maintained control with a strong system of government.

The Incas were skillful artisans, engineers, and builders. Ruins of great fortresses such as Macchu Piccu can still be seen. The stone buildings were built so skillfully that even without mortar the walls have withstood centuries of weathering and earthquakes. The hillsides of the Andes are covered with terraces designed by Incan engineers to aid in the irrigation of farmland. The stone foundations of Incan rope suspension bridges are still in use. Textiles recovered from Incan burial sites are colorful and beautifully designed. Metalworkers made beautiful ornaments and statuary from gold, silver, and other precious metals.

Inca society was agricultural, people living in extended family groups called *allyus*. The structure imposed by the Incan leadership gave each person in the culture a job to do. There was no monetary system, so commerce was a matter of trading and bartering, carefully controlled by the government. Taxes were paid in the form of goods and services. Every man was required to spend part of every year working on government construction projects or in the army. Other men in the allyu would take over farming and home responsibilities while he was gone. Part of all goods and food produced was given to the government. The government kept storehouses of food, weapons, and goods to support the Incan people in times of need.

The Inca empire came to an end with the arrival of the Spanish in 1532. Francisco Pizzaro and his men defeated the Inca leaders and easily took over the empire.

The Aztec—1250 to 1521 AD

The Aztec were a wandering people before they settled in the Valley of Mexico in the 1200s and ruled most of Mexico through the 1400s and early 1500s. According to legend they were instructed by their god to settle on an island in Lake Texcoco. There they built the magnificent island city of Tenochtitlan on the site of present day Mexico City.

By the 1400s the mighty Aztec armies had built an empire that covered much of southern Mexico. They had one of the most advanced civilizations in the Americas. Religion was extremely important in Aztec life. It inspired the building of towering temples and huge sculptures, but also required human sacrifices to feed its gods.

Aztec society was divided into three classes: slaves, commoners, and nobles. The emperor was called the *huey tlatoani* or Great Speaker. Although the emperor had great power, he had to consult with a council of nobles before making important decisions.

In 1519 the Spanish explorer Hernando Cortes landed in Mexico. The Aztec emperor, Montezuma II, did not resist the advance of the Spaniards because he believed Cortes to be the god Quetzacoatl. By 1521, the Spanish conquerors had destroyed the Aztec empire.

European explorers did not expect to find civilizations as advanced as the Maya, Inca, and Aztecs when they reached the new world. In their search for wealth and conquest, they were amazed by the many fascinating features of these three cultures. Pretend that you are a fifteenth-century explorer and have just arrived in the New World. Select one or both of the projects below to begin your journey into the world of these early Americans.

Project

Create a map that records your journey through Mexico, Central, and South America.

Materials

- Map page, following
- World map
- Colored pencils
- Fine-tipped marker
- Large sheet of butcher paper
- Tempera paint and brush or markers

Directions

1. Duplicate the map page for every student.

2. Using the world map, locate and mark:
   - Yucatan Peninsula • Cuzco • Mexico City • Andes Mountains

3. Using the color key on the map page, outline and color the areas occupied by the three civilizations.

4. As your study progresses, add the names of sites that were important to the Aztec, Inca, and Maya.

5. With paint or markers, create a large copy of the map page on butcher paper and mount on the bulletin board.

6. Fill in the map details with fine marker and use the bulletin board as a display area for projects related to your study.

Project

Plan a museum exhibit of Mayan, Incan, and Aztec artifacts.

Materials

- Student projects

Directions

1. Divide the class into three groups: the Mayas, the Incas, and the Aztecs.

2. As groups, organize an exhibit area for the projects completed during your study. Include information about the significance of the items on display.

3. Invite parents or another class to your museum exhibit and share your knowledge.

Inca, Aztec, Maya Map Activity

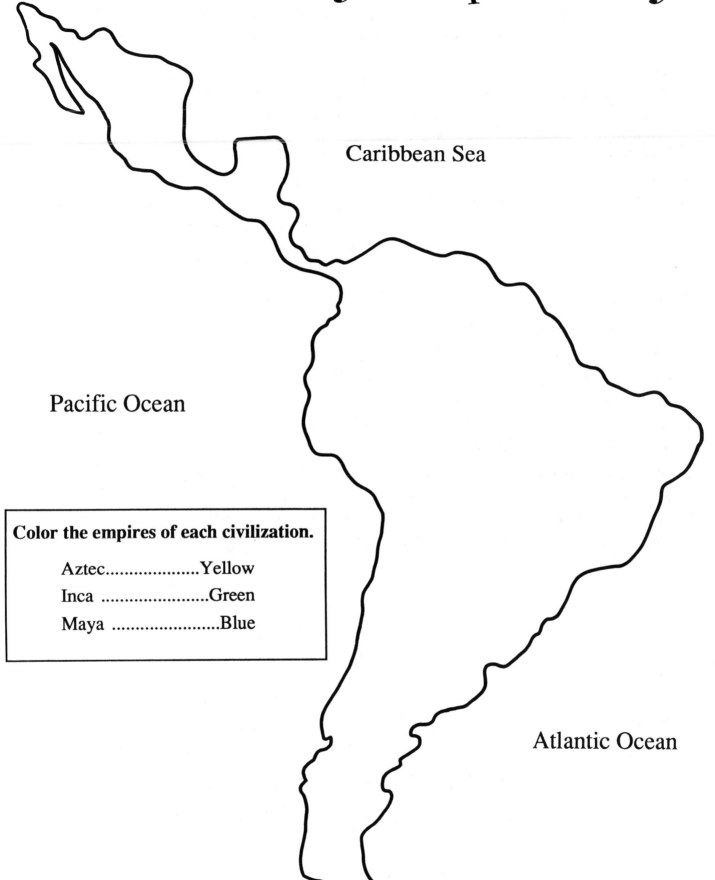

Caribbean Sea

Pacific Ocean

Atlantic Ocean

Color the empires of each civilization.

Aztec....................Yellow

Inca ....Green

Maya ....Blue

Stone of the Sun

One of the most important Aztec objects that has survived is the very elaborately carved *Calendar Stone* or *Stone of the Sun.* This massive, circular stone sculpture was discovered in 1790 beneath Mexico City's central square. It is four feet (1.22 m) thick, 13 feet (4 m) in diameter and weighs more than 24 tons (21.7 metric tons)!

The stone is edged with symbols for the 20 days of the Aztec calendar. In the center is the face of the sun god Tonatiuh with a protruding knife blade for a tongue. Other carvings on the stone are religious symbols related to the worship of this powerful god.

This stone was not just a calendar. It told when the world was supposed to have begun and when it would end. The Aztecs believed they were living in the fifth and final era. They believed that the four previous worlds had been destroyed by jaguars, hurricanes, volcanic fires, and torrential rains. The Aztec world ended far sooner than expected—with the arrival of the Spanish in 1519.

Project

- Study the beautifully detailed carvings of the Stone of the Sun while coloring the designs.
- Get a feel for its size with a measuring activity.

Materials

- Pattern page, following
- Colored pencils
- Tape measure

Directions

1. Reproduce the pattern to be used as a coloring page.

2. Try to identify the symbols for the Aztec months.

3. Look near the center of the stone. Try to identify the jaguars, hurricanes, fires, and rains—the destroyers of the earlier worlds.

How Big is Big?

1. Measure your height and the height of some friends. How many of you could lay end to end across the Stone of the Sun? Lay on the ground to demonstrate the size of this massive sculpture.

2. How much is 24 tons (21.8 metric tons)? If the average family car weighs about 4,000 pounds (1,814 kg), figure out how many cars you would need to equal the weight of the The Stone of the Sun.

Stone of the Sun

Aztec Symbols for the Months

Rain	Flower	Crocodile	Wind
House	Lizard	Serpent	Death's Head
Deer	Rabbit	Water	Dog
Monkey	Grass	Reed	Jaguar
Eagle	Vulture	Motion	Flint Knife

Writing

༺༺༺༺༺༺༺༺༺༺ Historical Aid ༺༺༺༺༺༺༺༺༺༺

The Aztec people had no alphabet. They used a form of writing called pictographic writing, which mostly uses little pictures to represent words. Some pictures symbolized ideas. For example, a drawing of a shield and a club meant "war." Other pictures stood for the sound of syllables. The Aztec town of Coatepec was represented by a picture of a snake and a hill because these two words together sounded like the name of the city.

It was difficult to use this kind of writing for stories. It was mostly used to keep business records, population counts, religious and historical writings, and tax lists.

Pictographs were painted on walls and vases, carved into monuments and sculptures, and kept in books called *codices*. These books were written on pieces of tree bark that had been varnished and stuck together to make long strips, some as long as 35 feet (10.6 m)! Priests trained as scribes would draw on both sides of the paper, making sure the important people were drawn larger than the others. The book was then folded like an accordion.

Project

Play an encoding game with a friend using pictographic writing.

Materials

• Paper
• Colored pencils
• Friend

Directions

1. Think about a message you would like to send to a friend.

2. Translate this message into pictographic writing using pictures to represent the words or syllables.

3. Give the message to your friend to decode. Did he or she need an answer key?

Marketplace

Historical Aid

The marketplace was a major center of Aztec life. Every village had at least one *tianquiztli*, a marketplace where goods of every description were bought and sold. These open air markets were lively, bustling places where people met to trade their excess goods for things they needed, catch up on the latest news, and visit with friends. Most markets were open at least five days a week .

It is believed that as many as 60,000 people attended the great market at Tlateloco every day! The market was very clean and orderly—all the stalls selling the same merchandise were placed together. Supervisors and judges regulated prices and dealt with thieves and cheaters.

Much of the buying and selling was done by exchanging products, called *bartering*. Cacao beans, cotton cloths known as *quachtli,* and small T-shaped pieces of copper were used as money.

Project

Do a math activity using Aztec money.

Materials

- Paper
- Pencils

Directions

1. Using the list of actual Aztec market prices from about 1520 AD as a starting point, brainstorm a class list of prices for other products found at a typical Aztec market— sandals, jackal and deer skins, maize and other produce, pitch for torches, pottery, salt cakes, tobacco, feathers, cloaks, gold, silver and precious stones, medicines, shells, and baskets.

2. Work in a group to make up a shopping list and calculate the bill. Trade your list with another group. Did both groups come up with the same total?

NOTE: 1 quachtli (cotton cloth) equals 65 cacao beans.

Aztec Market Prices in Cacao Beans		
1 turkey	=	100 beans
1 rabbit	=	100 beans
1 turkey egg	=	3 beans
1 fresh avocado	=	3 beans
1 tomato	=	1 bean
1 tamale	=	1 bean
1 fish wrapped in maize husks	=	3 beans
5 long green chilies	=	1 bean
1 obsidian blade	=	5 beans
1 cactus fruit	=	1 bean
1 log of firewood	=	1 bean

Clothing

Historical Aid

Aztec women wore a loose, sleeveless blouse and a wraparound skirt. Men wore a loincloth around their hips and a cloak knotted over one shoulder. The poorer people wore animal skins or clothing made from *maguey* fibers. The maguey plant has fleshy leaves that were used to produce wine as well as fibers that could be woven into a rough fabric for clothing.

Wealthier people wore cotton clothing. The cloth was produced by the women of the household. Even the wealthiest noblewomen helped in the making of cloth. First the raw cotton had to be cleaned and combed. Then the cotton was spun by hand into thread and the thread was twisted into yarn.

Solid cakes of different colored dyes could be purchased at the marketplace. After the yarn was dyed, it was woven into cloth. The amount of decoration on a finished garment usually indicated the wealth of the wearer.

Project

Make a traditional piece of Aztec clothing.

Materials

- Scissors
- White fabric or sheets
- Crayons
- Iron
- Needle and thread OR sewing machine

Directions

1. Cut fabric into pieces 24x48 inches (61 cm x 1.2 m) each.

2. Color a design on the fabric. Press hard on the crayons to get a bright color.

3. BOYS: Knot the fabric over one shoulder to form a cape.

   GIRLS: Fold fabric in half. Cut an opening for the head. Stitch the sides closed leaving a space for armholes.

Warriors

Historical Aid

Warfare was considered a religious duty and a normal part of Aztec life. Wars were fought not only to increase the size of the Aztec Empire, but to capture prisoners to sacrifice to the gods. The highest goal for a young Aztec man was to be a successful warrior. Showing courage in battle was the best and most common way to become successful. Men who took many captives in battle were rewarded with land, important government offices, and high social rank.

The chief weapon carried by Aztec warriors was a wooden club called a *maquahuitl*. Measuring about 30 inches (76 cm) long, this war club had grooved sides edged with sharp pieces of *obsidian* or volcanic glass.

For protection, warriors wore padded cotton armor and carried shields made of woven reeds and animal skins decorated with bright feathers. High-ranking warriors were awarded costumes with distinctive designs such as a jaguar or eagle suit and headdress.

Project

Make a scale model of an Aztec war club.

Materials

- Heavy cardboard
- Aluminum foil
- Glue
- Paint stirrer
- Paint brushes
- Scissors
- Stapler (optional)
- Tape
- Tempera paint

Directions

1. Cut two club shapes from cardboard. (See illustration.)

2. Tape folded pieces of aluminum foil along the side edges of the club to simulate the obsidian pieces used by Aztec weapon makers.

3. Glue the two halves of the club to the paint stirrer. Reinforce with staples, if necessary.

4. Paint to look like wood.

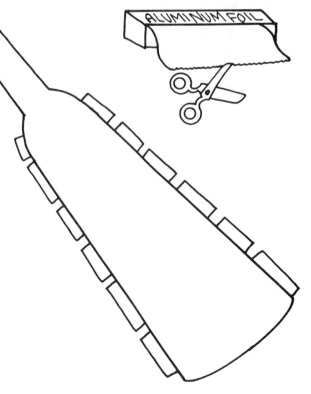

Agriculture

❧❧❧❧❧❧❧❧❧❧ **Historical Aid** ❧❧❧❧❧❧❧❧❧❧

Maize, or corn, was the most important crop grown by Aztec farmers. Other food crops included avocados, a variety of beans, sweet potatoes, pumpkins and other squashes, green and red tomatoes, peanuts, red, green and yellow peppers, many different types of chili peppers, herbs such as sage, cactus like prickly pear cactus, and vanilla beans.

The tropical climate of the lowland areas produced cotton, papayas, rubber, and cacao seeds (from which cocoa is made). Aztec farmers made clearings in the dense forests that covered the lowlands by chopping down the trees and then burning them. The ashes were mixed into the soil for fertilizer. This method of preparing land for farming is called *slash-and-burn* agriculture.

In the highlands, Aztec farmers created areas for planting by cutting terraces into the hillsides. They dug irrigation systems to aid in the watering of the crops. Shallow lakes were also turned into farmland. Mud from the lake bottoms was scooped up to form islands known as *chinampas*.

Project

Set up an exhibit featuring the various food crops grown by Aztec farmers.

Materials

- Index cards
- Marking pen

Directions

1. Using the historical information above, write the names of the different crops grown by Aztec farmers onto separate index cards.

2. Ask students to take a card home and bring in a sample.

3. Arrange the cards along with the sample products in a learning center for students to explore.

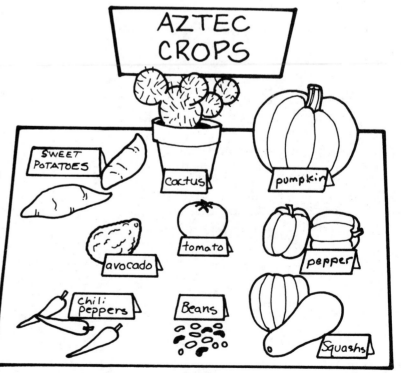

Chinampas

Historical Aid

The Aztec farmer grew many of his crops on *chinampas*—plots of land built in swampy lakes. Chinampas were begun by staking out narrow, rectangular strips in the shallow areas. Narrow canals were dug between the strips for canoes to pass through. The water plants cut from the surface of the lake along with the fertile lake-bottom soil were piled up in layers onto the rectangles to make plots of farmland. This resulted in a grid of narrow strips of land about 300 feet (91.4 m) long and 22 feet (6.7 m) wide, surrounded by canals. Willow trees were planted around the edge of each chinampa to make it more secure.

Farmers lived year round on their little islands. They could easily tend to their crops of flowers and vegetables by hauling buckets of water out of the adjoining canals and adding fresh mud dredged up when necessary.

In production all year round, chinampas could produce several crops annually. Without the need to constantly hunt for food, the people had time for arts, crafts, trade, and building.

Project

Sometimes called "floating islands," *chinampas* did not float at all! Make a diorama illustrating this method of farming.

Materials

- Heavy cardboard for a base
- Construction paper
- Tempera paint
- Paint brushes
- Pieces of foam or sponges
- Tape
- Marking pens, crayons
- Assorted craft materials such as felt scraps, pipe cleaners, tissue paper, etc.

Directions

1. Build a diorama—you might begin by drawing out a grid with pencil on the cardboard base just as an Aztec farmer might have done with stakes in the marshland!

2. Paint in the water. Add foam rectangles for the built-up areas.

3. Enhance your diorama by adding trees, crops, plants, farmers, and their homes.

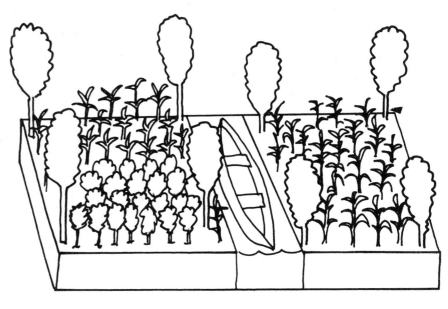

Arts & Crafts

Aztec

In the Aztec culture, a person's rank in society was measured by the quality and number of his possessions. The craftworkers who produced the beautiful items so desired by the nobility became highly valued members of the Aztec culture. The artisans formed special groups, called *guilds*, to set standards for payment and quality. There were over 30 different officially recognized craft guilds.

Metalworkers not only fashioned gold and silver into jewelry and religious ornaments, they also made copper into needles, fishhooks, and other essential tools. Stonecutters used these copper tools along with water and sand to shape precious stones into sacred objects and decorative pieces. Featherworkers created colorful headdresses, mantles, and shields. Sculptors carved stone into massive pieces over nine feet (2.7 m) high and tiny figurines less than an inch (2.54 cm) long. Potters shaped clay into beautiful vessels that were decorated with wonderful designs and colors.

Project

Learn about Aztec crafts by making some examples based on those created by Aztec artisans.

Materials

• See individual crafts on this and the following page

Sculpture

Aztec sculptors were known to craft snakes, jaguars, eagles and even grasshoppers and flies.

Materials

• Clay

Directions

1. Shape clay into a small figurine. You may wish to duplicate the grasshopper carving in the illustration.

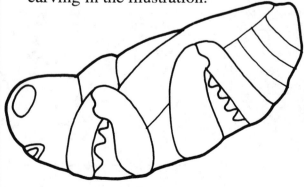

Pottery

Aztec potters built imaginative pieces. Examples include a pot shaped like a foot and another shaped like a sleeping dog!

Materials

• Heavy duty paper bowls   • Pencil
• Tempera paint   • Paint brushes

Directions

1. Paint a paper bowl in the style favored by Aztec potters. Painted decoration on pottery pieces was usually done in only two colors. A common design was based on an abstract pattern of zigzag lines.

Mosaics

Aztec artists made remarkably detailed mosaic ornaments and masks using bits of turquoise and shell.

Materials
- Poster board
- Pencil
- Glue or paste
- Scissors
- Construction paper

Directions
1. Sketch your design onto poster board and cut out.
2. Cut construction paper into small pieces. Glue onto your design to create a mosaic.

Featherwork

Featherworkers glued the feathers onto a piece like a fan individually. If they were working on a cape, however, they actually tied the quills to the fabric during the weaving process!

Materials
- Scissors
- Paper plate
- Paint stirrer
- Glue
- Crayons
- Construction paper

Directions
1. Draw a design such as a butterfly or flower in the center of the plate.
2. Cut out feather shapes from construction paper and glue around the outside of the plate. Glue onto a paint stirrer for a handle.

Metalwork

Gold and silversmiths produced beautiful ornaments such as necklaces of fine beads, masks, plaques, and earplugs.

Materials
- Scissors
- Paper
- Yarn or floss
- Glue
- Pencil
- Gold spray paint

Directions
1. Cut paper into long rectangles or triangles. Roll the paper over the pencil to form a bead. Glue down the end.
2. Have an adult paint your beads gold. String beads to form a necklace.

Featherwork

Aztec

Nobles and dignitaries in the Aztec culture dressed in stunning feather-covered garments and used large, circular, feathered fans. Aztec warriors wore elaborate suits covered with many varieties of brightly colored feathers. Even a warrior's headdress and shield were covered with layers of feathers worked into beautifully detailed patterns and designs.

Featherworkers began a project such as a fan by backing a sheet of cotton with leaves from the *maguey* plant. The fabric would be stiffened with glue, then stenciled with designs such as butterflies or flowers. Then the artist would use a bone spatula to glue the colorful feathers onto the stiffened material.

The crested *quetzal* bird is a brilliant green color on top and red below with long streaming tail feathers in the male. These iridescent feathers were the most prized by featherworkers.

Project

Make a "feathered" headdress that resembles that worn by an Aztec warrior.

Materials

- Poster board
- Scissors
- Stapler
- Sequins, glitter, foil paper, etc.
- Crayons or marking pens
- Feathers or feather shapes cut from construction paper

Directions

1. Cut a crown shape from tagboard to fit around the head.

2. Glue on an assortment of decorations including disks cut from foil, bits of feathers, etc.

3. Staple or glue on the feathers, creating a decorative design or pattern.

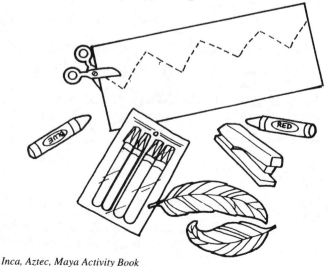

Music and Dance

Historical Aid

Music and dance were an important part of Aztec feasts and rituals. Solemn religious ceremonies as well as joyful feasts were livened up by the beating rhythm of rattles, whistles, flutes, shell trumpets, gongs, and drums.

Two different kinds of drums were played—a vertical drum and a horizontal drum, called a *teponaztli*. This drum was made out of a hollowed log with a hole in the bottom. Slits were cut into the top of the drum, and it was played with rubber-tipped drumsticks. Drums might be decorated with intricate carvings, painted, or gilded with gold.

Professional singers and dancers performed at sacred rituals accompanied by a small orchestra of musicians.

Project

Experience the feel of Aztec music and dance through a variety of activities.

LISTEN!

Aztec music was not very varied. The musicians had no stringed instruments and many of the instruments played only one note.

• Recording of all-percussion style music

Listen to music that is performed using all percussion instruments. Do you like the sound? If you were choosing music to listen to for a long period of time, would you prefer music with just a strong beat or music with a melody? Why?

RECITE!

After the ceremonies, people would attend parties in the homes of the wealthy. They would enjoy good food, music, plays, and poetry recited to the beat of drums and the music of flutes.

• Various percussion instruments
• Book of simple poems

Choose a piece of poetry. Practice with a group to beat out a tempo that matches the rhythm of the poetry.

PLAY!

Rattles were made of clay, metal, or large seeds strung together. They were made in all different shapes —even a dog's head!

• Macaroni or beans   • Small boxes
• Tape   • Tempera paint   • Brushes

Paint boxes with decorative patterns or designs. When paint is dry, add a scoop of beans or macaroni and carefully tape shut . Have fun playing your rattle to accompany a dance, reading, or musical performance.

DANCE!

Dancers attached strands of bones, shells and copper bells to their clothing which added to the beat of the music.

• Small jingle bells   • Yarn or ribbon

String bells onto ribbon. Wrap around your leg below the knee. Dance and listen!

Food

Aztec

❦❦❦❦❦❦❦❦❦❦❦❦ **Historical Aid** ❦❦❦❦❦❦❦❦❦❦❦

The main ingredient of the Aztec diet was *maize* or corn. A thin cornmeal pancake called a *tlaxcalle* was eaten at every meal. We know this food today by its Spanish name—*tortilla.*

Beans were second only to maize in importance in the Aztec diet. Tomatoes, avocados, prickly-pear cactus, sweet potatoes, and several varieties of squash were also eaten. Aztec cooking was rich and spicy and many dishes were flavored with chili peppers.

The Aztec diet consisted mostly of vegetables. Hunting provided a large portion of the meat which was eaten. Turkeys, ducks, and dogs were also raised for meat. Other sources of protein included insects, larvae, and cakes made from the blue-green algae collected from the surface of the lakes.

Project

Prepare recipes based on Aztec foods and have a tasting party!

Materials

• See individual recipes for ingredients and materials to prepare each dish

> *Tlaxcalli, or **tortillas**, were used to scoop up other food. Or the tlaxcalli was wrapped around vegetables and meat to form a taco.*

• Corn tortillas (See page 47)
• Cooked, chopped beef, turkey, or chicken
• Chopped tomatoes
• Jarred salsa
• Cooking oil

Heat oil in an electric skillet. *(Caution: keep hot oil well away from children.)* Briefly heat corn tortilla in oil. Stack on a plate. Fill your taco, fold, and eat!

> *Beans were a major source of protein in the Aztec diet.*

• One pound (453 g) dried pinto beans
• 6 cups (1.4 l) water
• 1½ tsp. (7.4 ml) salt
• 2 Tbsp. (30 ml) bacon fat

Cover beans with water. Simmer over low heat for 1½ hours. Add salt and bacon fat and continue cooking until beans are tender.

Recipes

Chocolate was considered by the Aztec to be a very special beverage. They even used cocoa beans as a form of money! The Aztec made their hot chocolate with water, cocoa, honey, and vanilla for flavoring.

- 2 cups (472 ml) milk
- 2 Tbsp. (30 ml) sugar
- 2 ounces (56.7 g) unsweetened chocolate, cut into small pieces
- ¼ tsp. (1.2 ml) vanilla

Heat all ingredients in a large saucepan over low heat until chocolate is melted. Whip vigorously with an egg beater until a good foam forms on top.

Squash seeds were eaten in many different ways. Try tasting seeds from a pumpkin which is a vegetable that originated in Central America.

- Pumpkin
- Salt
- 1 Tbsp. (15 ml) butter

Scoop out the seeds and pulp from the inside of a pumpkin. Wash and dry the seeds. Spread out on a cookie sheet. Add the butter and salt. Bake at 400°F (477.88°C) for 10 minutes. Stir to coat seeds with melted butter. Bake an additional 40 minutes at 300°F (148.88°C).

Colache is still a favorite vegetable dish in Mexico. This recipe goes back to Aztec times.

- 1 onion chopped
- 1 Tbsp. (15 ml) butter or margarine
- ½ cup (118 ml) water
- 1 cup (236 ml) green beans, cut into pieces
- 6 zucchini, cut into pieces
- 2 large tomatoes, cut into wedges
- 3 ears of corn, cut into 1-inch (2.54-cm) pieces
- 1 green pepper, chopped

Cook the onions in butter or margarine until golden. Add the beans and the water. Cook for 10 minutes. Add the zucchini, tomatoes, corn, and chopped green pepper. Cook, covered, until the vegetables are tender.

Ahuacatl, or avocados, are native to Central America. The Spanish explorers wrote in their journals about the nutty taste and buttery texture of this fruit they called aguacate.

- 2 very ripe avocados
- 2 tsp. (10 ml) chili powder
- 1 tsp. (5 ml) lemon juice
- Tortilla chips

Mash avocados until smooth. Add chili powder and lemon juice. Stir. Serve with chips.

Social Structure

Inca

Incan society was very structured. There were two noble classes under the Tapa Inca: *nobles by birth* and *nobles by privilege*. Nobles by birth included members of the Inca's family and anyone who could claim descendence from the original Inca. It was from this group that the Tapa Inca chose his governing group, called the Council of Nobles, and the governors of the empire. Nobles by privilege were leaders or chiefs of conquered lands or military heroes honored by the Inca. They were the local officials, or *curacas*. One curaca would be in charge of 100 *ayllus* and the curaca at the next level governed ten lower curacas. The governing pyramid finished with the region's governor and the Tapa Inca.

The basic social unit was the ayllu, which might be a group of related families or just local tribes. Each ayllu shared everything: livestock, land, food, beliefs. A foreman would be in charge of ten ayllus and reported to a curaca. Every person within an ayllu had a specific task assigned, depending on his age and sex. Old and young alike had work to do to support the community.

Project

Do a matching activity to learn the responsibilities of the different levels of Incan society.

Directions

1. Reproduce Inca Info Match-Up. Cut the Info section out as one piece and glue to the center of the construction paper.

2. Cut the answers apart on the solid lines.

3. Read each Info section and select the answer slip that matches it. Glue the answer next to the section it matches.

4. Compare answers with the rest of the class.

Materials

- Construction paper
- Inca Info Match-Up page, following
- Glue
- Scissors

Answer Key:

1. Coya	6. Inca Man	11. Governor	16. Inca Woman
2. Priest	7. Metalworker	12. Tapa Inca	17. Tapa Inca
3. Farmer	8. Chief Priest	13. Curaca	18. Priest
4. Architect	9. Council of Nobles	14. Builder	19. Tapa Inca
5. Noble by Birth	10. Weaver	15. Nobles by Privilege	20. Engineer

Inca Info Match-Up

1. Wife of the Tapa Inca, often his sister. The next Inca would probably be her son.	11. Chosen from the Nobles by Birth, he represented the Inca in one of the four sections of the empire.	**a. Council of Nobles**
		b. Farmer
2. Responsible for carrying out religious ceremonies and taking care of the temples.	12. The leader of the empire. His family was thought to be descended from the sun god.	**c. Architect**
		d. Nobles by Birth
3. Produced food for the empire. He farmed one field for the community, two for the government.	13. Official who oversaw 100 ayllus.	**e. Inca Men**
		f. Metalworker
4. Designed buildings , palaces, and temples. He was not required to pay taxes.	14. Constructed stone buildings so skillfully that no mortar was needed to keep them standing.	**g. Chief Priest**
		h. Priest
5. A member of the Inca's family or a descendant of the first Inca.	15. Leaders of conquered lands who continued to rule their own people as long as they followed Inca custom.	**i. Weaver**
		j. Engineer
6. Required to perform service in the army, on construction projects, or working in the mines.	16. Required to weave a length of cloth in payment of taxes.	**k. Curaca**
		l. Tapa Inca
7. Made jewelry, ornaments, and statues from gold and silver. He did not have to pay taxes.	17. Wore his clothing only one time.	**m. Builder**
		n. Tapa Inca
8. Brother of the Tapa Inca who oversaw the work of the priests in the empire.	18. Used divination to make decisions about daily life.	**o. Coya**
		p. Priest
9. Helped the Inca rule the empire.	19. Was responsible for being certain that everyone in the empire had what they needed.	**q. Inca Woman**
		r. Nobles by Privilege
10. Made beautiful textiles from cotton and wool. He did not have to pay taxes.	20. Designed elaborate irrigation systems on terraced hillsides.	**s. Tapa Inca**
		t. Governor

The Tapa Inca

Historical Aid

The Incan culture took its name from its leader, the Tapa Inca, the "divine ruler" or "direct descendant of the sun." The Tapa Inca would have many wives, his chief wife being called the *coya*, or empress. His heir would usually be a child of the coya.

The coronation of a new Tapa Inca was celebrated by days of feasting. A new palace was always built, as the old palace contained the mummy of the previous Tapa Inca. The palace walls were plated with sheets of gold and silver.

The Tapa Inca wore clothing made from the finest cottons and wools and never wore a garment more than once. He wore huge earplugs, large golden disks decorated with jewels, and ate from plates and cups made of gold and silver. Any food he left uneaten was saved, and once a year it was burned along with all of his used clothing. The Tapa Inca rarely walked, but was carried by litter-bearers.

Project

Make a *borla*, the headdress worn by the Inca.

Materials

- Yarn in a variety of colors, including red
- Scissors
- Tubular penne pasta, painted gold

Directions

1. Cut several lengths of yarn in a variety of colors. Holding them together, fit the strands around your forehead and tie together at the back.

2. Cut twelve strands of red yarn, four inches (10 cm) long. Divide yarn strands into six pairs.

3. Taking each pair of yarn strands singly, tie one end of each pair to the front of the headdress.

4. String a piece of gold-painted pasta onto each pair of yarn strands. Take the untied ends of two yarn pairs and tie them together under the pasta, leaving a fringe.

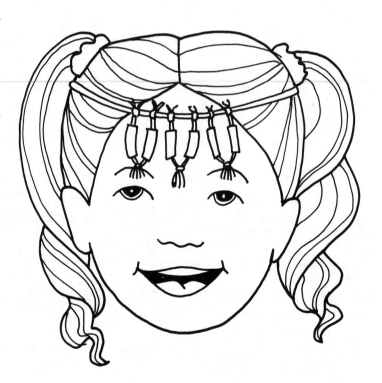

Language

Historical Aid

The ancient Incas spoke a language called *Quecha* (KESH-wa). Descendants of the Incas still speak the same language today. As the Incan empire expanded, absorbing the lands of the tribes around them, the Incas insisted that the captured tribes learn Quecha as their primary language.

The Incas never developed a written language, so much of what is known about their culture has come down from stories passed from one generation to the next. Because there was no writing system, important information was spread by way of messengers, or *chasquis* (CHAZ-kees), who would run along the royal roads with important news of the empire.

Project

Play a game and relay messages as the Incas did.

Materials

- Playing field area
- Identical message written on a separate piece of paper for each team
- Paper and pencil for each team

Directions

1. Divide the class into teams. The first member of each team positions himself on one edge of the playing field. The last team member stands on the other edge of the field, directly opposite the first team member. The last team member is given a pencil and paper.

2. The remaining team members place themselves in a line between their first and last team members, spreading out so that they are equidistant from one another.

3. The first member of each team is given one of the messages. On a signal, he reads the message to himself and puts the paper on the ground. He runs to the next player on his team, relays the message verbally, then goes back to his spot.

4. When he is back in place, the next player runs to relay the message. The message is passed down the line until it reaches the last player. The last team member writes the message he receives on his paper and sits down.

5. The written message is compared to the original message. Points are given for finishing order and for correctness of the message.

Religion

Inca

XXXXXXXXXXXXX **Historical Aid** XXXXXXXXXXXXX

The religion of the Incas was based on agricultural gods. Their primary god was the creator, *Viracocha*. He was assisted by gods of the sun, moon, stars, thunder, earth, and sea. It was believed that the emperor's family was descended from the sun god, *Inti*. Large temples were built in the cities and were taken care of by priests. The Inca considered many places and things sacred.

Religion and ceremonies were an important part of Incan life. Priests began each day with prayers, divination, and offerings. Large ceremonies were held on special calendar days, and were marked by dancing, feasts, games, songs, and parades.

It was believed that the will of the gods could be determined by divination, or the reading of magic signs. Divination methods included the study of animal organs, flames of a fire, or the movement of animals. No decision was made without divination, whether it was a government decision or a decision about when and where to plant crops.

Project

Use a coin as a divination tool to determine a walking route.

Materials

- Coins
- Parent or other adult help
- Paper or a simple map of the area
- Marker

Directions

1. Divide into groups, assigning an adult leader for each group. Each group will need one coin and a map or piece of paper for tracking the group's route. Assign one person to mark the route as you go.

2. Determine the length of time that your walk will last. All groups begin at the same time and place.

3. A member of each group flips a coin. If it falls heads, the group goes to the right; if it falls tails, they go to the left. Repeat this step at every corner reached. Be sure to accurately mark the turns made, including street names.

4. At the end of the determined time, return to the starting point to compare walking routes.

Life After Death

Historical Aid

The Incas believed that after they died they would live in another world. Therefore, they were buried with many of the things that they would need in the next life. When the Tapa Inca died, his body was kept in the palace he lived in during his reign and a new palace was built for the new Inca. Often the ruler's servants and wives would volunteer to die to be kept with him in the world to come.

Bodies were mummified and wrapped. The body would be bound in a flexed position with rope, then wrapped in cloths. The mummy was seated upright in its tomb and surrounded by goods. Mummies were looked after just as if they were still living. People would consult their dead for advice. Mummies of emperors were brought out and paraded during ceremonies.

A mummy would be decorated according to the status of the person who had died. Nobles and emperors would be wrapped in fine cloth, and often adorned with jewelry, precious metals, and fine burial masks.

Project

Make an Incan mummy-mask.

Materials

- Heavy-duty paper plate
- Brown tempera paint and paint brush
- Small shells and/or mosaic tiles
- Black or brown yarn
- Two-inch (5-cm) wide strip of colorful fabric
- Large gold buttons
- Glue   • Hole punch

Directions

1. Paint paper plate with brown tempera paint.

2. Punch holes at half-inch (1.27-cm) intervals along the top and bottom edges of the plate (forehead and chin).

3. Glue shells and tiles to the plate to design a face with detailed eyes and mouth. Glue buttons onto mask as earplugs.

4. Cut long strands of yarn and tie into the punched holes to make hair and a beard. Tie the fabric strip around the top of the head like a head band.

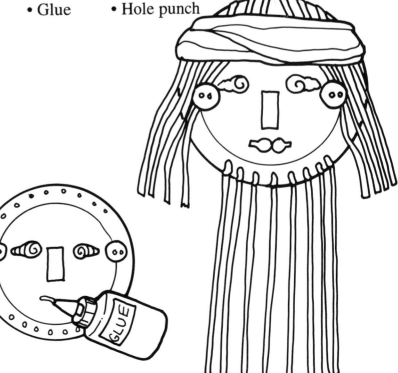

Inca. Aztec. Maya Activity Book

Quipu

Historical Aid

One of the things that made the Inca civilization so successful was its ability to maintain control over the widespread empire. In order for the government to be sure that taxes were being paid and that everyone's needs were being met, information had to be relayed from one end of the empire to the other, all without written records.

One recording device used by the Inca was the *quipu*. The quipu was used to count the population, keep track of what they produced, and to maintain records of supplies kept in government storehouses The quipu was made of pieces of string or cord in different colors tied onto a base cord. Different colors or types of knots would record various kinds of information. The quipu was kept and interpreted by a *quipu-kamay-us*, a "master of the knotted cord."

Project

Make and use a *quipu* to record class information.

Directions

1. Decide on a topic on which to take a class survey. For example, take a survey of what pet(s) each student has. Brainstorm a list of possible answers. Select a quipu-kamay-us to keep the record.

(Alternate: provide yarn for each student to make his own quipu.)

2. Select one color yarn for the quipu base, and a different color for every answer category (e.g., blue for dogs, orange for cats). Tie the category colors to the base.

3. Name a category to be counted and ask students who fit the category to stand. Count the number of students.

4. The quipu-kamay-us ties knots on the appropriate quipu string to correspond with the number of students.

Materials

• Yarn in a variety of colors, cut in two-foot (60-cm) lengths

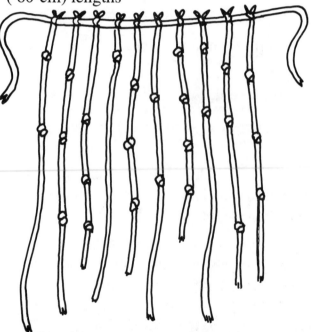

Quipu knots: The Incan accounting system was based on tens. The knots tied furthest from the base strand were the ones. Next would come a space, and then the knots for tens, then hundreds. For example, the number 134 would be represented by four knots at the end of the strand, a space; three knots and a space; one knot. An absence of knots was zero.

Transportation

Historical Aid

The Inca traveled and transported goods almost entirely on foot. They had not discovered the wheel, so they did not use carts or any other form of wheeled transport. Llamas were often used to carry goods, but were not ridden. The Tapa Inca and noblemen often traveled on a *litter*, a chair supported by poles, carried by men called litter-bearers.

The roads in the Incan empire were paved and well maintained by government work parties. *Tampos*, government-built inns, were spaced at a distance of a day's travel along the roads. Only people on official government business were allowed to use the roads.

The steep hillsides of the Andes presented a problem for Inca travelers: deep gorges and canyons to be crossed. The Incas became skillful builders of suspension bridges made of rope or strong vines. The rope would support a rush matting footway. Each end of the bridge would be firmly anchored on a stone foundation, many of which are still used as bridge supports today.

Project

Have a litter-bearer relay race.

Directions

1. To make sedan chair, use cord to tie the dowels to the arms of the chair. Center the chair on the dowels so that both ends of each dowel can be held.

2. Divide the class into teams. Divide each team into pairs.

3. Have a relay race in which each pair of players carries the stuffed animal in the sedan chair to a designated line and back. If a pair loses their passenger, they must go back to the starting line.

4. The first team to complete the race successfully wins.

Materials

For each relay team:
- Chair with arms (a lawn chair would be suitable)
- Two wooden dowels, about four feet (1.2 m) in length
- Sturdy cord
- Large stuffed animal

Weaving

Inca

Historical Aid

Textiles woven by the Incas were colorful and beautifully patterned. Fabrics were woven of cotton or wool from the llama or alpaca. Finer wool came from the vicuna, and was reserved for the nobility. Dyes were made from minerals or plants. All women were required to weave. They wove textiles for the use of their family or for trade, and their textiles were used as tribute or taxes paid to the emperor.

Weaving was done on portable back-strap looms. One end of the loom was attached to a stationary object; the other end looped around the weaver's body. Warp threads ran lengthwise between the two sections of the loom; the weft threads were woven over and under, across the width of the warp. A heddle stick and shed rod were used to lift the warp threads as needed, and a weaving sword was used to smooth weft threads. Patterns were created by using additional heddles or by lifting different sets of warp threads.

Project

Learn to use a back-strap loom and weave a piece of fabric.

Materials

- Two one-inch (2.54-cm) dowels, 12 inches (30 cm) long
- Yarn in a variety of colors
- Cord or narrow rope
- Plastic yarn needle

Directions

1. Decide on combination of yarn colors, and cut lengths of 18 inches (46 cm).

2. Tie one end of each yarn length to one of the dowels, very close together. Tie the other ends of the yarn strands to the second dowel (warp threads).

3. Cut two 24-inch (60-cm) lengths of cord and tie one to the end of each dowel.

4. Anchor one of the dowels to a stationary object such as a playground pole or a tree by looping the cord around the object and tying it to the other end of the dowel.

5. Repeat with the second dowel, looping the cord around your body at your waist. Sit, then move back until the yarn lengths are fully extended.

6. Thread a long strand of yarn through the needle (weft strand). Weave the needle over and under the warp yarn. With your fingers, gently push weft yarn toward the bottom dowel. Continue back and forth across the warp yarns, tying new yarn strands onto the weft yarn as you run out or as you want to change colors.

7. Work until you reach a length of about 12 inches (30 cm). Carefully untie the yarn strands from the dowels, tying the yarn pieces to each other to secure.

Clothing

Historical Aid

The Inca people wore simple clothing woven from llama or alpaca wool or cotton. The emperor and the nobility used finer wools from the vicuna. Each person had two sets of clothing—one plain for everyday use, and more colorful clothing for ceremonies and special days. The amount of decoration depended on the person's social status.

Men wore a loincloth held by a woolen belt, covered by a sleeveless tunic. Over that they wore a woolen cloak that was also used as a blanket. Men always carried a small pouch over the shoulder to hold personal possessions. Women wore long tunics covered by woolen cloaks that were fastened at the shoulders with metal pins. Both men and women wore sandals or went barefoot. On their heads they wore hats knitted from wool or cotton.

Each tribe had its own distinctive hairstyle that included combs, ribbons, and other ornaments. Members of the nobility wore more elaborate clothing and decoration. They also wore jewelry and gold arm bands and had golden decorations sewn on their clothing.

Project

Make a pouch like those used by Incan men.

Directions

1. Fold bottom edge of fabric or construction paper strip up 4½ inches (11.4 cm). Staple in place along both edges. Fold the top edge over to form a flap.

2. Cut 36-inch (1-m) lengths of several colors of yarn. Twist or braid them together and tie the ends to form a loop.

3. Lay a section of the yarn loop underneath the flap and tape flat. Close the flap over the yarn.

4. Thread the yarn needle with a 12-inch (30-cm) length of yarn. Push the needle through the bottom folded edge of the pouch and pull until one end of yarn is free. Pull both ends of yarn to make them even. Tie a knot close to the edge, leaving the ends free. Repeat across the bottom to make a fringe.

Materials

- Strip of fabric woven on back-strap loom (previous page) or construction paper cut in 4x12-inch (10x30.5-cm) strip
- Yarn in various colors
- Yarn needle
- Crayons or markers
- Scissors
- Tape
- Stapler

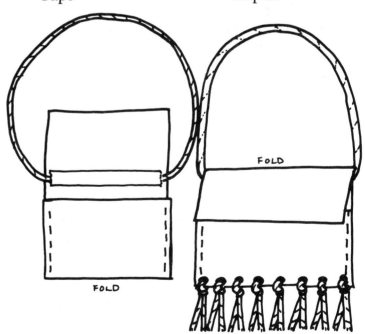

Craftsmen

Inca

There are many examples of the skilled craftsmanship of the Inca. Artisans were highly respected and did not have to pay tribute to the emperor. Their art was their contribution to the community.

Samples of cotton and woolen textiles that have survived are richly colored and have beautiful, complex designs. Incan ceramics were very striking. Designs on their pottery show details about Incan life that we would not otherwise know. Metalworking in Peru began 3,500 years ago. Incan metalsmiths worked with gold, silver, platinum, and bronze. Garments and ornaments were made and decorated with the colorful feathers of tropical birds by skilled featherworkers.

Project

Create an Incan pot, feather fan, necklace, or statue.

Materials

See individual projects

Pottery

The Incas were master potters. Pottery vessels were used for ceremonies and for daily use. Pottery made for everyday use was often simple, but ceremonial pots were usually richly decorated, often with animal shapes or with designs carved in the pottery. Pottery was not made on a wheel, but with stacked coils of clay.

Materials

- Self-hardening clay
- Acrylic paints and brush
- Pointed orange stick (as used for nail care)
- Protected work surface

Directions

1. On work surface, make a round disk of clay to use as the base of the pot.

2. Roll long coils of clay and begin building the sides of the pot, winding the clay one layer on top of the one below. When the sides are the desired height, use your fingers to smooth the clay.

3. Use additional clay to decorate the pot, or use the orange stick to carve designs into the clay.

4. Allow the clay to dry, then paint, if desired.

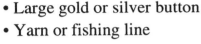 # Metalworking

Gold, silver and other precious metals were used for ornaments, jewelry, statues, and ceremonial objects. Gold could be worn only by the emperor and the nobility. Gold was hammered into thin sheets and used to cover palace walls. Jewelry included large earplugs and necklaces. Precious stones such as jade and turquoise were also highly valued.

Materials

- Gold or silver-painted macaroni
- Green and turquoise-painted macaroni
- Large gold or silver button
- Yarn or fishing line
- Scissors

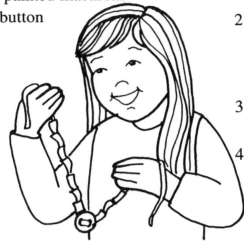

Directions

1. Cut a length of yarn or fishing line to fit comfortably over the head.

2. String macaroni on the yarn, creating a pattern. Thread the button on the yarn at the center of the necklace. Continue threading the macaroni.

3. Tie the two ends of the yarn together to form a necklace.

4. Allow the clay to dry, then paint, if desired.

Featherworking

Feathers were used to make or decorate many practical, everyday objects. Fans such as this one were used to cool people on hot days. The most popular feathers came from macaws and parrots.

Materials

- Construction paper in bright colors
- Brown yarn
- Scissors

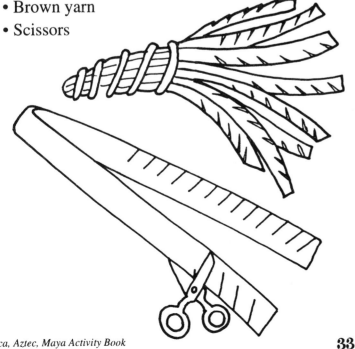

Directions

1. Cut construction paper lengthwise into strips about two inches (5 cm) wide. Fold each strip in half lengthwise.

2. Keeping it folded, snip each strip at close intervals along the cut edge about three-quarters down the length of the strip.

3. Open the strips and run the edges between your fingers to "feather."

4. Gather the uncut ends of the feathers together. Wind yarn around the bunched ends and tie off.

Food

Inca

The diet of the Inca consisted mainly of vegetables, sometimes with the addition of guinea pig or fish. The emperor and the nobility had more variety in their diets. They ate a wider selection of vegetables, and also ate meat such as llama or fish. A common meal would consist of a vegetable stew containing potatoes, okra, beans, tomatoes, and squash, seasoned with salt, herbs, and pepper.

The Inca's primary crops were maize and potatoes. The maize would be toasted, boiled, or ground into flour to make bread and cakes that were baked on a hot stone. The Incas were the first civilization to grow potatoes. The potatoes would be stored in caves high in the mountains where they would freeze. By alternating the freezing with air-drying, the Incas developed a method of freeze-drying that would preserve the potatoes for long periods of times.

Project

Make and sample a vegetable stew.

Directions

1. Wash fresh vegetables. Slice the okra and the zucchini. Cut the potatoes into small chunks.

2. Combine the vegetables with the canned tomatoes and green beans in the pot. Cook slowly until the potatoes are tender. Season with salt and chiles to taste.

Materials

- Large soup pot
- Knives
- Can opener
- Plastic spoons
- Wooden spoon
- Cutting board
- Disposable bowls

Ingredients:

- Two large cans of diced tomatoes
- Four potatoes
- Two cans green beans
- ½ lb. (227 g) fresh okra
- Two medium zucchini
- ½ small can chiles (optional)
- Salt to taste

The Mayans

Historical Aid

Maya people were short. The average height of the men was five feet one inch (155 cm). Women averaged four feet eight inches (142 cm). Their skin was coppery or brown. Their hair was straight, black, and long. The men wore braids wound around the top of their head and a ponytail hanging down in back. Women wore their hair in a variety of styles.

They reshaped their bodies to create features they valued. Heads were bound at birth between two boards to create a forehead that was flattened and sloped back. Children wore a bead that hung from their hair over their forehead and between their eyes. Focusing on the bead caused their eyes to eventually cross. Front teeth were filed to sharp points with pieces of carved jade often placed into them.

Body painting was also valued. Warriors painted their bodies black and red; young men painted themselves black until they married. Priests and people who were to be sacrificed were painted blue. Prisoners were painted with black and white stripes. The curves of the face and body were decorated with colorful tattoos.

Project

Work in cooperative groups to make life-sized models of a Mayan man and woman.

Materials

- White butcher paper
- Fabric and assorted craft supplies
- Tempera paints and brushes
- Pencils
- Scissors
- Stapler
- Newspaper
- Measuring tape
- Glue
- Black yarn
- Construction paper

Directions

1. Divide into small groups.

2. Measure each person in the group to find members the same height as the average Mayan man or woman. You may need to borrow a member of another group!

3. Have your "Mayans" lay on the butcher paper. Trace around their body. Make two outlines per person to create a front and back. Cut out the body shapes.

4. Staple the front to the back and stuff lightly with crumpled newspaper.

5. Paint, dress, and add details to the shapes according to what you learn about the Maya in your studies.

Daily Life

Maya

The ruling classes and the elite did not work at everyday chores, but for the common Maya families, the days were long and hard. The women rose and started the fires before four o'clock in the morning. They made breakfast, toasting leftover cornmeal tortillas. (See page 47.) By five o'clock the men had eaten and left for the fields with their sons, who were learning to farm. They returned mid-afternoon, hunting along the way with spears and clay pellets. When not working the fields, the men labored to build temples, pyramids, other buildings, ball courts, and roads. After a bath and dinner, they worked at making wooden or jade articles, some of them to trade.

The women washed, cleaned, and ground the corn they needed for the two daily meals they cooked. They swept their homes, cared for their children and tended to their animals— ducks, turkeys, and an occasional monkey. They gathered cotton and did spinning and weaving to make clothes. The women had hot baths ready for the men when they returned. After dinner, they continued their spinning and weaving.

Children did not go to school. Their parents taught them skills which they used to help with the daily chores. At the end of the day, all retired to sleep on woven mats.

Project

Plan and carry out a simulation of Mayan daily activity.

Directions

1. Provide each participant with a Mayan Daily Schedule.

2. Discuss what you know about Mayan daily life.

3. Complete the schedule as instructed at the top of the form. Discuss and assign all material needs.

4. Make a "master copy" of the schedule on the poster board to display the day of the simulation.

Materials

• Mayan Daily Schedule, following
• Poster board
• Marking pens, pencils
• Materials as needed for simulation

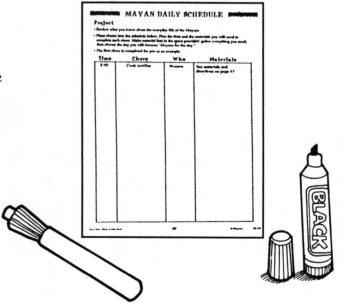

▧▧▧▧▧▧ MAYAN DAILY SCHEDULE ▧▧▧▧▧▧

Project

• Review what you know about the everyday life of the Mayans.

• Place chores into the schedule below. Plan the time and the materials you will need to complete each chore. Make material lists in the space provided; gather everything you need; then choose the day you will become "Mayans for the day."

• The first chore is completed for you as an example.

Time	Chore	Who	Materials
8:00	Cook tortillas	Women	See materials and directions on page 47

Calendar

Historical Aid

Mayan priests used mathematics and astronomy to develop two kinds of calendars. One was a sacred almanac of 260 days. Each day was assigned one of 20 day names and a number from 1 to 13. Each of the 20 day names had a god or goddess associated with it. Mayan priests made predictions of good or bad luck by studying the combinations of gods or goddesses and numbers. Based on these predictions, the Maya noted those days that would be lucky for activities such as farming and hunting.

The Maya also had a calendar of 365 days based on the orbit of the earth around the sun. These days were divided into 18 months of 20 days each, plus 5 days at the end of the year. The Maya considered these last five days to be extremely unlucky. During that period they fasted, made many sacrifices, and avoided any unnecessary work.

Project

- Conduct a comparison activity.
- Create a good luck calendar.

Materials

- Several current calendars
- Good Luck Calendar, following
- Crayons
- Pencil

Directions

1. Divide into small groups. Give each group a current calendar. Compare the calendar with a 365-day Mayan calendar.

2. Reproduce the Good Luck Calendar for each student.

3. Write the name and dates to correspond with the current or upcoming month. Color the Mayan decorations on the calendar page.

4. Predict lucky days and mark them with a crayon. Track predictions throughout the month. Allow time daily to discuss events you think were brought about by good luck.

LUCKY CALENDAR

Sunday	Monday	Tuesday	Wednesday	Thursday	Friday	Saturday

Recreation

Maya

Historians estimate that the Maya worshipped more than 160 gods and goddesses. Among them they worshipped a corn god, a rain god, a sun god, and a moon goddess. Religious festivals in honor of particular gods took place on special days throughout the year. In fact, these religious festivals provided one of the favorite forms of recreation for the Maya. During the festivals there was much dancing and feasting.

Another favorite activity was a religious game that resembled basketball. The specially-designed court represented the world. The ball stood for the moon and sun. Ballplayers wore helmets, gloves, thigh guards and a thick protective belt. The players scored by hitting a solid rubber ball through a stone ring with their elbows or hips. Many bets were placed on the outcome of the game!

Project

Play a modern version of a Mayan ball game.

Materials

- Rubber ball
- Playing field
- Plastic hoop

Directions

1. Go outside to a playing field. Divide into two teams. Choose a captain for each.

2. The captain bounces the ball to a player on his or her own team. The player tries to use an elbow or hip to bounce the ball through the plastic hoop held horizontally about five feet (1.5 m) away by two people from the opposing team. The hoop must remain stationary or a penalty shot may be retaken. Score a point for each successful rebound.

4. Alternate teams until each player has had at least two chances. Total the points.

Music

Historical Aid

Music and dancing were important parts of Mayan religious festivals. Music was the background for chanting prayers, for reciting the myths and legends of the people, and for hundreds of different ceremonial dances. Instruments were crafted from natural resources. There were not stringed instruments, only percussion and wind instruments. Drums were made from hollow logs, tortoise shells, and clay, in every size and shape. Other rhythm instruments included bells, gourd rattles, and human and animal bones that were tapped or rubbed against each other. Flutes and trumpets, made from conch shells, wood, and clay, carried the melody.

If a musician missed a beat, the punishment was severe. The dancers, sometimes numbering in the hundreds, were also punished if they missed a step. There were groups of men dancers and of women dancers, but they rarely danced together. Some dances were rituals to bring rain; others pictured wars and daily happenings. Dancers wore magnificent costumes and three-foot high (91.4 cm) headdresses.

Project

Craft a musical instrument or choreograph a Mayan dance.

Materials

• Variety of resources as determined by students

Directions

1. Review the materials used in Mayan instruments and the purpose of a dance.

2. With this information in mind, work with classmates or on your own to create a musical instrument or dance. Gather resources from home, school, or outdoors. Be imaginative.

3. Assemble all musicians and dancers when all projects are complete. Practice playing in a group. When the band is ready, the dancers may perform. Don't miss a beat!

Communication

Maya

The Maya developed an advanced form of writing consisting of many symbols. These symbols represented combinations of sounds or entire ideas and formed a kind of hieroglyphic (picture) writing. These symbols were used on stone monuments and books of paper made from fig tree bark to record information about religious ceremonies, important events, and astronomy.

Mayas also used a mathematical system based on the number 20 instead of 10 as in the decimal system. Dots and dashes represented numbers, and a special symbol represented zero. Mathematicians consider the zero one of the world's greatest inventions and they credit the Mayans for this accomplishment.

Project

- Invent and play a card game based on dots and dashes instead of numerals.
- Create a desk-top name plate using picture symbols.

Math Game

1. Brainstorm as a group to create sets of dots and dashes that represent numbers.

2. Use marking pens to write the new numbers on an equivalent chart. Post the chart on the wall.

3. Work in groups of four to make playing cards. Refer to the chart and write a "Mayan" number on an index card. Make four cards for each number.

4. Shuffle the cards and play a game similar to "Go Fish."

Materials

Math Game
- Writing paper
- Pencils
- Index cards
- Poster board
- Marking pens

Name Poster
- Crayons
- 12x6-in (30x15-cm) white poster board folded in half lengthwise
- Alphabet Picture Chart, following

```
1 = • • -
2 = - • -
3 = - - • •
4 = - - -
5 = - • - -
```

Symbol Writing

Project

- Study the chart below. Find the letters of your first name. Practice writing your name in the space at the bottom of the page.
- Use crayons to rewrite your name in big, colorful picture symbols on each side of the folded poster board. Set your name plate on your desk.
- Look at the example. Can you read the name?

A a	B b	C c	D d	E e
F f	G g	H h	I i	J j
K k	L l	M m	N n	O o
P p	Q q	R r	S s	T t
U u	V v	W w	X x	Y y
Z z				

Clothing

Maya

The clothing of the Maya kept them comfortable in the hot tropical climate. The men wore a loincloth, a strip of cloth tied around their hips and passed between their legs. Sometimes they wore a square of cotton around their shoulders. Women wore loose dresses that reached their ankles. These garments were woven from cotton or other fibers. The people of the upper class wore finer clothes decorated with brilliantly-colored embroidery and ornaments.

Elaborate headdresses, jackets, and loincloths were made of the brightly-colored feathers of jungle birds. Mayans also created mosaics by weaving feathers into cotton fabric. Sometimes they were tied or pasted in. Only priests, chiefs, and important warriors could wear the golden-green feathers of the quetzal because of the high cost.

On their feet, the Mayan men wore hemp or deerskin sandals with two thongs that passed between the toes. They also made shoes from latex. (See page 46.) Women wore sandals only on special occasions.

Project

Create a feather mosaic.

Directions

1. Cut feathers from tissue and construction paper in different sizes and colors. Be sure to make the valuable golden-green feathers of the quetzal!

2. Cut slits in the cloth. Weave the paper feathers through the slits. Glue other feathers in place.

Materials

- 12-inch (30.5-cm) fabric square
- Tissue and construction paper in assorted bright colors
- Fabric scissors
- Fabric glue

FABRIC GLUE

Jewelry

Historical Aid

Maya men and women wore a great deal of jewelry. Priests, nobles, and other members of the elite wore the same kind of jewelry with more elaborate designs. On their heads they wore earplugs, lip plugs, and nose ornaments. Besides necklaces they also wore bracelets, rings, pendants, and bands that circled their knees and ankles.

Mayans crafted their jewelry from numerous natural resources. Teeth from the jaws of crocodiles or the revered jaguar were common materials, as were shells, obsidian (a natural glass that sometimes forms when lava cools quickly), bone, and wood. They particularly favored jewelry made from gemstones. Jade was the most precious material because it was associated with water, the life-giving fluid, and with the color of the maize plant, their staple food. They also liked other stones with shiny surfaces. Turquoise, onyx, rock crystal, and porphyry (a dark red rock) were common resources.

Project

Design and create Mayan jewelry.

Directions

1. Select paper to represent the type of gemstone or other materials used by the Maya to make jewelry. For example, use white to simulate animal teeth or green to represent jade.

2. Decide which type of jewelry to make—necklace, bracelet, ring, ankle band, etc.

3. Cut, roll, crumple, or fold the paper to make different shaped beads, teeth, or shells.

4. String the paper beads, teeth, or shells to create the type of jewelry you decided on.

Materials

- Magazines
- Scissors
- Yarn, string
- Plastic stitchery needles
- Construction, crepe, and tissue paper

Rubber

Historical Aid

The rain forest in which the Maya built their civilization provided an excellent environment for rubber trees, which flourish in hot, moist climates. Mayans, along with other Latin American Indians, were the original users of rubber. They learned how to tap the rubber trees for latex, a milky white juice that oozes from the bark.

Latex was used to make a number of products. Bouncing balls were used in sacred ball games (see Recreation, page 40). Waterproof bottles were made by smoothing latex on a bottle-shaped clay mold. The latex was dried over a fire. The clay was washed out leaving a hollow shell. The Maya also made waterproof shoes from latex by spreading it on their feet and letting it dry.

Project

"Fashion" a pair of Mayan rubber shoes.

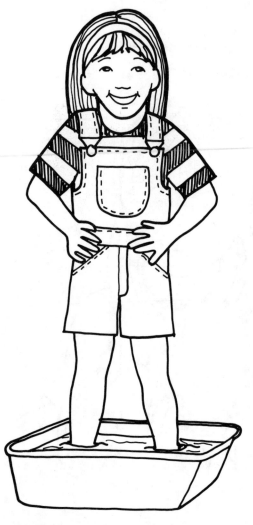

Materials

• Flour
• Water
• Paint stirrers or wooden spoons
• Large tubs
• Plastic sheet or other drop cloth
• Towels

Directions

1. Mix flour and water in tubs. Blend enough water to make a thin paste. The mixture should be about ankle high.

2. Take off your shoes and stand in the tub. Step out onto the drop cloth.

3. Wait for the mixture to dry. While your new "shoes" are not waterproof, it is easy to understand how the Maya made their shoes from rubber.

4. Wash the feet and dry with towels.

Food

Historical Aid

The Maya's chief crop was maize, or Indian corn. They also raised black and red beans, squash, pumpkins, chili peppers, tomatoes, avocados, papayas, and sweet potatoes. But corn was a part of every meal every day of their lives, and it was sacred to them. War was fought only after the corn had been harvested!

The corn was prepared by soaking the kernels overnight in pottery jars then grinding it by hand with a stone on a stone slab. Breakfast consisted of cornmeal pancakes, called *tortillas,* roasted over a fire. In the fields the men nourished themselves by mixing two or three lumps of corn dough with water to make a milk-colored drink. Dinner included black beans, and if the hunting had been good, roasted meat or a stew of rabbit, deer, or turkey. Sometimes there was meat from a tapir, armadillo, or turtle.

Chocolate, from cacao, was a favorite hot drink. They also made a drink spiced with bark and sweetened with honey from the honeybees raised in their farmyards. The women of the family never ate with the men. They served first and ate their own meals later.

Project

Make and sample tortillas.

Materials

- 1 cup (236 ml) instant masa
- ½ cup (118 ml) water
- Medium bowl
- Plastic wrap

Directions

1. Place masa in a medium bowl. Work in water with your fingers to make a soft dough. If dough is crumbly mix in a little more water.

2. Shape dough into a ball. Cover with a damp towel; let stand 20 minutes.

3. Place plastic wrap on a flat surface. Divide dough into 20 equal pieces. Place another piece of plastic wrap on top of the dough and press with the palm of your hand to flatten. Remove plastic.

4. Preheat an ungreased griddle over medium heat. Cook tortillas on each side until lightly spotted with brown.

Makes 20 3-inch (7.6-cm) tortillas

Arts and Crafts

⌘⌘⌘⌘⌘⌘⌘⌘⌘⌘⌘ **Historical Aid** ⌘⌘⌘⌘⌘⌘⌘⌘⌘⌘⌘

The Maya were excellent painters, potters, and sculptors. Mayan artists made small sculptures of clay and carved huge ones from stone. Most of the small sculptures were figures of men and women, although gods and goddesses were also a favorite subject. The large sculptures, some of which stood more than 30 feet (9 m) high, were carved with figures of important persons in stiff poses. Large stone monuments, called *stele*, were sculpted with picture-writing symbols and depicted important events in the lives of their rulers and their rulers' families.

Mayan artists decorated walls with brightly colored murals that featured lifelike figures taking part in battles and festivals. The artists outlined the figures and then filled in the various parts with color. They rarely shaded the colors. This painting style is also seen on Mayan pottery.

Project

Complete a painting or clay project.

Materials

• As listed for each project

Mural

Materials
• Crayons
• White construction paper

Directions
1. Color a picture with bright colors using the techniques and subjects described in the information section.

2. Assemble the pictures side-by-side on the wall to form a mural.

Sculpture

Materials
• Self-hardening clay
• Toothpicks • Craft sticks

Directions
1. Create a small sculpture using the techniques and subjects described in the information section.

2. Use toothpicks and craft sticks to sculpt detail. Allow clay to harden.